# Whispers of the Heart

Vijetha Kambli

BookLeaf Publishing

India | USA | UK

Presentation by *BookLeaf Publishing*

Web: www.bookleafpub.com

E-mail: info@bookleafpub.com

ISBN: 9789360940973

First edition 2024

*For all who feel deeply, and for those who find solace in words…*

*and*

*For all the women in my life who inspire my every word and every heartbeat…*

*I couldn't do life without you…*

# Life Got in the Way

I woke up at dawn with a thought on my mind,
Wondering how you were and if you were fine;
I wanted to call you, I really really did,
But then life got in the way and the opportunity was
rid.

I thought of you this morning, wondering if you were
okay,
Wondered what you might be doing, wondering how
had been your day;
I wanted to call you, but I knew I just wouldn't,
Life got in the way and I simply just couldn't.

You crossed my mind around noon, I found a smile
on my face,
Your silly antics and phrases, just things time can't
replace;
I wanted to call you, to share and laugh with you out
loud,
But then life got in the way, and I wasn't allowed.

This afternoon I was thinking, how much fun it
would be,
To just simply hang out, or the world together see;
I wanted to call you, maybe plan a vacation,
But life got in the way and all else is a placation.

This evening what was it, it was something
somebody said,
And hand on my heart, I couldn't get you out of my
head;
I wanted to call you, hear you say it too,
Bloody life got in the way, and there was nothing I
could do.

This night, oh this night, damn, what can I say,
You are on my mind and you just won't go away;
I want to call you, I want to call you so bad,
But this effing life is in the way, and I'm inconsolably
sad

It doesn't matter the time, it doesn't matter what I do,
You are on my mind, I can't not think of you;
I so want to call, I need to talk about so much,
I need to hug you, need to hold you, I just need your
hands to touch.

I need to see your face, I want to hear your voice,
I need to know when I have news, you are with me to
rejoice;
I want to be your rock, I need you to be mine,
When things get rough for either of us to know it will
be fine.

I want to take a long slow walk, down memory lane,
Talk about times good or bad or just to entertain;
But it doesn't matter what I want, or what I have to
say,
'Cause I can't even call since fucking Life got in the
way.

# Find Love

The improbability underscored by pride,
Experience points to risk;
Emotions tend to cloud the view,
With a blurry hazy mist.

Futility raised by reason,
Pain reminded by fear;
Loss echoed by grief,
Making decisions further unclear.

Odds calculated by the mind,
Past stressing on cost;
Ego raised by vanity,
Has you only further lost.

But possibility is sparked by hope,
Memories remind of glee;
The eyes remind you of all the magic,
In everything you might see.

Faith helps you stand upright,
Courage helps you start;
"Just give it a shot, you might find the stars,
Go find love," tells you your heart.

# Magic

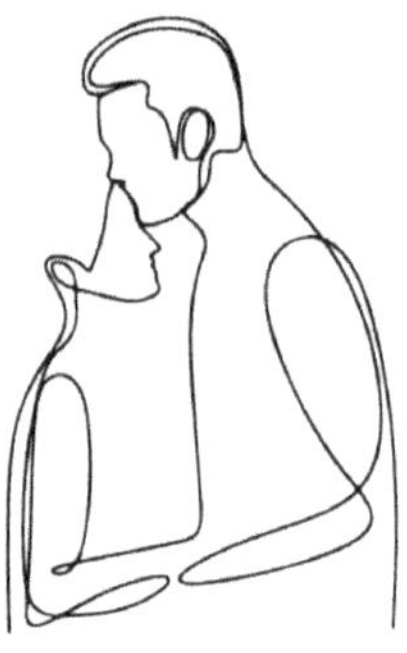

A four-car garage, a bank full of cash,
Success beyond compare;
A house by the beach, 65-inch tv,
An attitude with some flair.

A trip or two around the world,
People to know your name;
Threads that reflect your accomplishments,
And not-so-subtle fame.

Possessing everything you desire,
Owning everything you want;
Childhood dreams now fulfilled,
A wish that no longer haunts.

Everyone has these thoughts,
Each of us makes these plans;
But years pass by and we realise,
Not everything's in our hands.

Sure we might find our rainbow,
We might've made our dreams come true;
Maybe some, or maybe all, but still
Something stays missing inside of you.

People come and people go,
We learn to make our peace;
Build our walls and lock doors tight,
Open feelings tend to cease.

Yet something always will stay off,
Niggling emptiness inside;
Till you accept the all but universal truth,
From your heart to not hide.

Admitting the common thread we share,
At the root of it all we learn;
Success, fame, money mean little,
When there's one more thing we yearn.

A hug, a kiss, a gently held hand,
A single look in the eye;
The touch of breath against your skin,
A reminder that someone's nearby.

A reassuring presence to back us up,
A prop for should we fall;
A catalyst that propels ahead,
A strength that helps stand tall.

A kind word on a difficult day,
A reprimand when we need;
A marriage of lips, of bodies, of minds,
An escape, a haven, a reprieve.

A promise of a potential future,
An ever-evolving possibility;
A moving target of more joy, more bliss,
An aspiration of what can be.

An accomplishment like none other,
A sense of being complete;
A crown jewel, a cherry on a Sundae,
Gratification not victory or defeat.

Cause no matter what we each may do,
Unfinished remains our soul;
The magic of life doesn't ever compare,
'tis the magic of love that makes us whole.

# Will it Happen to Me?

Someone whose eyes light up,
Each time into mine they see;
Someone whose heart just skips a beat,
Will that ever happen to me?

Someone who texts "just because,"
Calls to check on how I may be;
Someone who just can't wait to meet,
Will that ever happen to me?

Someone who aches for my touch,
Or makes plans incessantly;
Someone who has hopes and dreams,
Will that ever happen to me?

Someone who has sleepless nights,
When my temperature rises by three;
Makes me soup and holds my hand,
Will that ever happen to me?

Someone who understands my soul,
And my heart's aching plea;
Someone who gets who I really am,
Will that ever happen to me?

Someone who wants to spend the time,
Travel the world or just watch telly;
Someone who wants to be there,
Will that ever happen to me?

Someone who will be my rock,
Set my weary self free;
Someone who will stand by my side,
Will that ever happen to me?

I don't see it yet, but hope I hold,
I believe in the powers that be;
Someday I will find my someone,
And my someone will indeed find me.

# Manifest

If I were an artist, a masterpiece I'd paint,
If I could, I'd sing an epic song;
A ravishing 7-course meal I would cook,
If in a kitchen my skills belonged.

If I were a musician, I'd play a tune,
Enchanting melodies just for you;
If I could sculpt, now it won't take a genius,
To guess what I would do.

I know these lines make little sense,
I'll explain in a moment or two;
I'm trying to say you deserve something special,
Something as unique as are you.

So here I am with a jar of words,
Stringing them together on this page;
To tell you in the only way I know how,
That like wine you get better with age.

You have a light that all can see,
That comes from the inside;
It draws those around like moths to a flame,
It's a glow you cannot hide.

A manner that's both gentle and kind,
Hiding 'neath a tough outer shell;
A demeanour seeming light and frivolous,
But a mind that thinks deep as well.

A laughter that though may be rare,
The most joyous sound one could hear;
A warmth that simply emanates,
For all to bask-in when they're near.

A voice that can be firm and soft,
A heart as pure as can be;
A soul that seeks and desires the divine,
Within spirituality.

A Code of Honour as solid as a rock,
Commitments held with pride;
Passion that just blooms and grows,
Faith that won't subside.

So many things both big and small,
Make you the man that you are;
In my own little way, I wanted to show,
That you shine like the brightest star.

Strong, fierce, loyal, loving,
Generous, kind and funny too;
Sweet, serious, sensitive, and silly,
Just more words to describe you.

I'll hit pause now and leave it be,
Just one last thing to say;
This person I doth manifest,
May the Universe send my way.

# Forever kind of Love

The kind that we read about in tales of yore;
That makes you smile like never before.
The kind that puts a pep in your step;
Erases trauma past; the kind you won't regret. The
kind that brightens up your day;
The kind that hurts whenever away.
The kind where discord is merely a blip;
Where there's joy in making up for it.
The kind that for no reason makes you smile;
That keeps growing and growing even after a
while.The kind where you can still be you;
Where one looks for things together to do.
The kinds that's silly, pure, and true;
The kind that's encouraging and forgiving too.The
kind that opens up your heart;
The kind you kinda knew right from the start. The
kind like these, a cut above;
I want a forever kind of love.

# Unravelled

Have you ever met someone,
And an instant connection felt?
Surprised by this force of nature,
This hand destiny has dealt?

Have you ever heard their voice,
Echo in your soul;
As inexplicable as it may be,
It somehow made you whole?

Have you hung on every word,
Agreed with all they had to say;
Understood their thoughts, their points of view,
How life made them think that way?

Have you ever lost track of time,
Not wanting to be apart;
A pull, a tug, an invisible cord,
A connection, a visible spark?

Have you caught yourself lost in thought,
Or staring at the phone;
In a room full of people but without them,
Felt utterly alone?

Have you ever admonished yourself,
For this isn't who you are;
What is this absurd obsession,
You're better than this by far?

But you can't help these feelings you feel,
The sensation of unhindered bliss;
The knowledge of finding something so rare,
An opportunity too good to miss.

Till time passes, the fog clears,
And you wonder if it was real;
The pain of it slipping through your fingers,
Too too much to deal.

Euphoria unravelled, colours paled,
Waking up to another day;
Wondering if it was a dream, a whim,
Or was it real and they got away?

# Have you?

Have you ever loved somebody,
Truly loved with all your heart;
So much that every day you've wished,
You could've been around from the start.

Have you ever loved somebody,
So much that it hurt inside;
Ever loved somebody so much that,
It became impossible to hide.

The world became a beautiful place,
Every colour seemed more bright;
The big blue sky, the gleaming sun,
Annoying birds now a beautiful sight.

Have you ever loved so much,
That you looked forward to each day;
People seemed to smile so much more,
Magic in what they have to say.

Have you ever loved so much,
All you want to do is make them smile;
Spent your life looking for that someone special,
To realise they were in front of you all the while.

So much that you can't be anything but grateful,
For grace that has been shown;
You thank your fate, your lucky stars,
Feel like the most blessed person ever known.

Have you ever loved so much,
That none else matters anymore;
You shield them from things dark and grey,
For them nothing you wouldn't endure.

Have you ever loved so deeply,
That you cry yourself to sleep at night;
You wish that person such true joy,
Even if it meant giving up the fight.

Have you ever loved so truly,
That even though it would break your heart;
You can bring yourself to walk away,
You convince yourself from bliss to part.

Have you ever loved in a way,
You never imagined you could feel;
Has life ever changed so much,
That you couldn't believe that it was real.

Have you given that place in your heart,
You never thought you'd give away;
Have you felt that constant knot in your stomach,
Though you see that someone every day.

Have you ever loved so much,
That you'd gladly even give up your soul;
For you are nothing without that someone,
Without that someone you are not whole.

Have you, have you, have you been so lucky,
To feel a love of this kind;
If you have, none can be luckier than you,
For such a love is hard to find.

Hold it close, don't let go,
Such grace is seldom if ever shown twice;
Hold on to it no matter what,
Don't worry 'bout consequence or price.

For if you ever love someone,
So much like I said above;
Trust me, friend, you've got it all,
You, dear friend, have found "true love."

# Musings

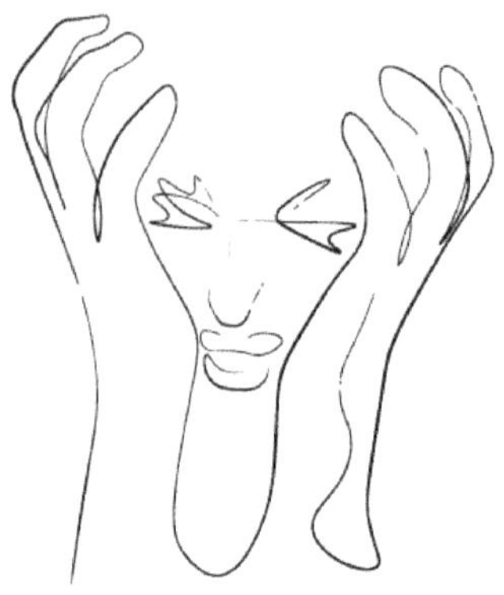

It doesn't matter how bright the sun,
Doesn't matter how pretty a day;
It doesn't matter the fresh-cut grass,
Doesn't matter that butterflies play.

It doesn't matter the children's voices.
It doesn't matter a rainbow in the sky;
It doesn't matter colours of the world,
Doesn't matter birds that fly.

It doesn't matter hues of twilight,
Doesn't matter the twinkling stars;
It doesn't matter reassuring moon,
Doesn't matter the magical hours.

It doesn't matter those near or far,
Doesn't matter which day;
Sometimes nothing, just nothing can matter,
Sometimes, life just feels that way.

No rhyme, no reason, no trigger, no cause,
No explanation of any kind;
All that matters is you know "this too shall pass"
It's but a musing of a dark mind.

# Tapestry of Life

Christmas has come and long since gone,
The once decorated tree now stacked away;
The cheer of new year now a memory,
Left to be recalled another day.

With every moment that passes by,
We have one less moment to live;
But I wonder with every smile that's shared,
Do we end up with one smile less to give?

Every storm is followed by calm,
Every high does have its low;
Joy and cheer are followed by a tear,
For it has nowhere else to go.

But does that mean each time our eyes twinkle,
With bated breath we wait;
Wondering when the axe will fall,
Wondering what shall be our fate.

Is it truly inevitable I ask,
That with a shining sun a cloud must loom;
Is this the real rule of this world,
Each celebration shall precede gloom.

If so then my question is,
Is happiness worth all the pain;
Is it a price we're all willing to pay,
Knowing wounds are all that will remain.

Is a bloom worth the thorn on its side,
A summer shower a lightning strike;
The beautiful ocean with its relentless waves,
Pretty mountains and their treacherous hikes.

Would you really want to smile,
If your heart was filled with fear;
Of impending doom, inevitable gloom,
And the agony of a falling tear.

I wonder, I wonder, I really do,
And while the answer I may never find;
The yin-yang of life does bear heavy,
On both my heart and on my mind.

# Love

Love isn't about just hearts and flowers,
It isn't sonnets and songs;
It's putting in the work, putting in the hours,
It's knowing where your heart belongs.

Love isn't about just fancy holidays,
Nor is it gestures grand;
It's a stolen moment in a crowded room,
It's as simple as a held hand.

Love isn't surprises and gifts and presents,
Nor unending shopping sprees;
It's remembering how many lumps of sugar,
A conversation that flows with ease.

Love isn't about public declarations,
Facebook, insta wherever else it may be;
It's an unexpected text just because,
It's the way in their eyes yourself you see.

It's acceptance, appreciation, admiration, and awe,
It's an alliance, affinity, and attraction;
It's all-encompassing, and all including,
Making you the goal, not a distraction.

Love is a gentle touch of the lips,
Hooked pinkies as you cross the road;
Love is your soda refilled in the fridge,
It's real plans, not just dreams of growing old.

Love is about sleepless nights,
While tending and providing care;
Love is knowing bad times will be better,
'Cause of the very love that's there.

Love is all these things and so much more,
The essence of all that may be;
Love is a promise, it's hope, it's faith,
That a better tomorrow we shall see.

# Beautiful

You are beautiful just the way you are,
A phrase to be heard each day;
A prayer, a chant, a war cry, a fact,
An echo, a loop, a mantra we should say.

That bumpy nose, the uneven hairline,
The thinner half of your lips;
The freckled skin, the tiny nails,
The too wide or too narrow hips.

The neck either too long or short,
The boobs too big or small;
The asymmetry of your face,
The worry lines or hair fall.

The thighs too thick or legs too thin,
The feet you find too large;
The shoulder round or too sharp,
The disappointing décolletage.

The thing you wish, the flaws you count,
The inches desired less or more;
The unsatisfying image you find in the mirror,
The one you pray you didn't abhor.

Definitions, parameters, gauges, opinions,
Meant to weigh you down so you won't be free;
To hold you back, to birth self-doubt,
Hypocrisy of the patriarchy.

Don't dismiss when those you love,
Tell you how pretty you are;
Don't try to diminish the light within,
'cause you can't diminish a star.

Don't reject a compliment,
Don't ignore what you see;
Don't focus on what you think is wrong,
Please just heed my plea.

For you, for me for all we know,
A reminder that we all need;
You are perfect my dear, you are Precious,
You're as *beautiful* as beautiful can be.

# Unfinished

The days seem both long and short,
I can't seem to figure out which;
I feel like I don't quite fit in,
Like an anomaly, a glitch.

A stranger in my own skin,
Unfamiliar and unknown;
Uncertain of today, more so of tomorrow,
Amidst people yet so alone.

A feeling I can't seem to shake,
An unending sense of dread;
I think, I hope, I manifest each night,
Waking up to despair instead.

It's not as if life has been unkind,
No, life hasn't been unfair;
I am grateful for all that I am,
I am lucky, I am aware.

Family, success and friendship, the kind
That stories are written about;
Skill, talent, opportunity and grace,
Yet my heart remains filled with doubt.

Of a life that's not quite lived,
A dream not realised;
A heart that hasn't quite loved,
An ache that won't subside.

A puzzle missing a piece, an unfinished painting,
An incomplete song;
A story that remains unfinished,
Like me that doesn't belong.

# A Prayer

Voices in my head that won't quiet down,
If anything seems louder now;
Stronger than the deepest of logic,
Superseding all my knowledge somehow.

From a once quiet whisper, they have grown,
Found strength and confidence;
Dark and twisted, and full of gloom,
They gnaw at my innocence.

They tell me time and time again,
Even though it's rough;
That it doesn't matter what I do,
I will never be enough.

Don't want to believe it but it's hard,
As much as I try to fight;
Truth is; the doubts keep creeping in,
At dusk 'n' through the night.

I wish I knew just what to do,
How I should evolve to be;
So that for once just somebody,
Would actually choose me.

For once in my life I wish it were true,
People stopped playing games and just saw you;
For once in my life I wish it could be,
Love being more than a stray fantasy.

For once in my life my hand would be held,
Hopes and dreams together would meld;
For once in my life as he touched my skin,
I'd feel the calm rise from within.

For once in my life together we'd dream,
A future of tomorrows—impossible as they seem;
For once in my life confident I'd be,
That as hard as it gets he won't abandon me.

For once in my life hugged and held tight,
Amidst the everyday crazy knowing it will be alright;
For once in my life my burdens to share,
To not be the one to always be there.

For once in my life cared for and not caring,
For once in my life not doing the sharing;
For once in my life protected and adored,
For once in my life no longer ignored.

For once in my life supported not supporting,
For once in my life expressing and emoting;
For once in my life the star of the story,
For once in my life basking in my own glory.

For once in my life I wish love I could find,
To truly seize someone's heart, soul and mind;
For once in my life if happy I could be,
Someone to whom I mattered and someone who
mattered to me.

# Life

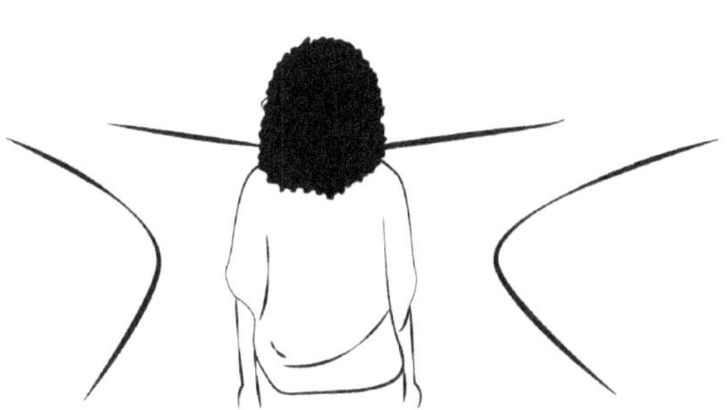

I've walked along the crossroads of life,
People have come and gone;
I've lent my shoulder, I've been a friend;
I don't have the strength to carry on.

I've smiled with tears welling up inside,
Laughed while my heart cried out in woe;
I've patiently listened and given direction,
While I knew not where to go.

I've put all lives much above mine,
Most everyone made the priority list;
Somewhere along the way I lost me,
'twas my name I seem to have missed.

Guess I believed that the way that I
Picked up those who were left behind;
Someone would notice I was missing too,
And then stop for me and try to find.

I held many hands, hugged many souls,
Helped them understand the Universe did care;
Reassuring them they had nothing to fear,
That no matter what I'd always be there.

The word 'no' has never existed,
For I always did all that I could;
There's nothing that I'd ever decline,
You just had to ask and you knew I would.

I have tried with all my might,
To be a messenger with grace from above;
I've tried to spread the word of peace,
Have tried to spread the word of love.

There's none that I'd keep anything against,
No grudge that I still hold;
I forgive, I forget, and truly believe,
What you give you receive tenfold.

Today I find myself distressed,
For I question my very belief;
And I seek answers fervently,
Till I find them there's no relief.

A friend of mine mentioned today,
That what you give is what you get;
And though that's what I once believed,
'tis a belief I now regret.

For the angst that does fill my life,
I do not think I could deserve;
I've never so much as hurt a flower,
Then why should I judgment reserve?

How can one ever justify,
The volume of pain that has been mine;
For all I've done is love and care,
Was that actually my true crime?

Was not love God's message,
Was not His teaching for us to care;
Was it not He who taught us sacrifice,
Wasn't it Him who told us to share?

 If that is true, if that is right,
All I've done is follow His trail;
Then where are my share of smiles,
Why do tears still prevail?

I sigh a sigh of deep remorse,
One that breaks my heart in two;
For life has but let me down again,
And I know not what to do.

Feeble, weak and vulnerable,
That best describes my state;
Reduced to just next to nothing,
All I can do is curse my fate.

Though answers I may never find,
What I do know is this;
I've spent my life sharing love and joy,
Gifting people moments of bliss.

Beyond that I know not how things work,
How the calculations of karma are made;
I give up, let go, and just live my life,
That brings me to the end of my tirade.

# Can Love Last?

With the passing of each moment,
With the turn of each day;
With every tick of that clock on the wall,
Can love fade away?

With each wave that does hit the shore,
Every leaf that falls to ground;
With every gush of listless wind,
Can love become a distant sound?

With every beat of a gentle heart,
Every bat of an eyelid;
With every move of every arm,
Can love turn but languid?

With each flower that blooms at dawn,
With each swing that chooses to sway;
With each turn of the merry-go-round,
Can love choose not to stay?

The stars that continue to twinkle each night,
With the moon that plays hide-n-seek;
With the welcome and adieu of every season,
Can love turn bleak?

With tomorrows becoming our todays,
And with todays joining the past;
With history constantly in the making,
I ask, can love really last?

# The Journey

For all the hardships and all the pain,
All the times I felt insane;
For all the grief, the painful tears,
And all the lonely lonely years.

For all the prices that were paid,
For all the dreams my will forbade;
For all the cold and lonesome nights,
For all the woesome hapless plights.

For all the sadness all the ache,
For all the times my heart did break;
For all feelings of being weak,
For the future that seemed bleak.

For all the deep gut-wrenching cries,
For all the hate, for all the lies;
For all the people that did betray,
For all of those who walked away.

For all the times that ripped my heart,
For all the ends before their starts;
For all the things that crushed my soul,
For all the times I thought I'd never be whole.

For everything that was dark and grey,
For times I thought there wouldn't be a way;
For the endless tunnel that was my life,
For the lack of hope for the lack of light.

For everything and everyone,
For all the grief to be bourne by one;
I always, always questioned why,
Why was this destiny mine to try?

I now know 'twas my burden to bear,
For at the tunnel's end light was always there;
I just couldn't see it I had a ways to go,
I had my cross to shoulder, I just didn't know.

Now that I know, I have found my sun,
The clouds are gone, I am free I can run;
My skin is warm, the world is bright,
There's nothing around me but colour and light.

My lips now move in a different direction,
Found myself confused by this new affliction;
Till I discovered it was the feeling of bliss,
I was wearing a smile, I just didn't know this.

My heart felt full, my soul at peace,
Laughter, my only emotional release;
I am so grateful, I feel such debt,
There's nothing in my life that I regret.

For everything my journey was,
It wasn't one without a cause;
'twas but my path to find my cue,
My destination, my reward, my peace, my due.

# The End

You wish for just one more call,
You wish for a wayward glance;
You wish for a new memory,
You wish for a second chance.

You wish for but one more touch,
You wish for one embrace;
You wish for something, anything more,
You wish this emptiness replaced.

You wish, you wish, and wish some more,
But sometimes it's all they'll ever be;
shooting stars or pennies in wells,
Can't change reality.

Sometimes there just is no more,
No hugs, or kisses, to get;
Sometimes all there is to fill emptiness,
Is a big fat load of regret.

Regret over so many "what ifs,"
Of chances that weren't seized;
Regret of the sense of hopelessness,
That reality has besieged.

Sometimes that's all you're left with,
Sometimes that's all there'll ever be;
Sometimes as much as you may want more,
You're just left with the debris.

Sometimes the only place to find reprieve,
Is in our minds and dreams;
Sometimes no matter how hard we try,
Fate simply intervenes.

As much as you might please and pray,
Unto the universe vibes you may send;
Sometimes destiny still makes a call,
Sometimes it's just over—The End.

# All I want is You

In the silence of the moments,
In the quiet of my every day;
It's like a distant whisper,
Haunts me more than words can say.

An etch, an unerasable mark,
A shadow that's but here to stay;
A tattoo, a scar, a constant reminder,
An echo, an unending ricochet.

A musing of when you were here,
A provocation of how things used to be;
A phantom limb, an ache, a throb,
A joy, a wish, a fantasy.

Your words, your smile, your quirks, your touch,
Your laugh, your temper too;
Sounds, sensations, surreal interpretations,
Of everything that made you you.

I miss it all, every single one,
I miss you every day;
Grief grips my heart, and strangles my soul,
Doesn't feel like it'll go away.

How am I to overcome this sting?
How am I to quell this burn
To find a path that won't destroy me whole,
When there's just one thing for which I yearn?

Is not remembering, the only way ahead?
Create a fugue-like reality?
Is the only way to look beyond,
To not recall a 'you and me'?

How do I forge a path?
How do I create a future new?
The real question is—Do I want to forget it all,
When all I really want is to remember you?

# If

If I no longer call to say hello,
Send a text just because;
Don't share a thought that crossed my mind,
Or point at your silly li'l flaws.

If I don't ever walk by your place,
Or send you a greeting on a special day;
If I don't ask you how you are,
Or ask you to come by my way.

Will you be able to ever forgive me,
Do you think you can find it inside;
To accept the truth that I no longer care
To talk, to share, to confide.

Even if I don't lend an ear,
Nor offer a helping hand;
If I don't take you out to eat,
Or play with you in the sand.

What about if I return no calls,
Never again 'tis that I write;
I don't so much as even seem to care,
Concern not even in sight.

Do you think you'd forgive me then,
Though I'm no longer who I used to be;
Though my presence is just barely felt,
Turning into a distant memory.

What about if you wake up one morn,
And found that I'm not there;
That while you walk through my 'bode,
Emptiness fills the air.

You step into my li'l garage,
And my car's parked where it has been;
But the dust settled on it is evidence that,
Daylight it has not seen.

What if you try to call my phone,
And the number ceases to be;
And as hard you continue to try,
Just cannot reach me.

What if you cry and you realise,
That I can't wipe away your tear;
That as much as you might hope and pray,
I'm no longer near.

What if the only way you know I exist,
Is by hugging my teddy bear tight;
Hoping to meet me in your dreams,
While you go to sleep at night.

What if I'm gone, what if I end,
What if I cease to be;
Tell me the truth, tell me truly,
Could you forgive me?

# Again

I count the years and months and days,
Has it already been that long;
I pull up my calendar on my phone,
Cause I'm sure I must be wrong.

Of course, my phone tells me I'm not,
And it's as true as it can be;
Your number's still first on my contacts list,
The one I would've called in an emergency.

I think of you every day,
I miss you with all my heart;
I read our texts and look at pictures,
Wishing we were never apart.

You visit me often in my dreams,
Your advice rings in my ears;
In you, it is that I find my strength,
It is with you I assuage my fears.

I wonder what you would've said,
Wonder what you might've done;
I wonder about so many things,
If time we could've outrun.

I hope that you are at peace,
I hope you are proud;
I hope I can do you justice,
Even though you can't say it out loud.

I hope someday that we shall meet,
I hope you hold me again;
I hope you know how much I love you,
Namaha, Ameen, Amen.